Kindled Soul Holy Fire

In His Perfect Love ~
Donna Dwork
Jeremiah 32:17

DONNA OSWALT

Kindled Soul Holy Fire

LENTEN MEDITATIONS AND PRAYERS

Providence House Publishers
WWW.PROVIDENCEHOUSE.COM
FRANKLIN, TENNESSEE

Copyright 2009 by Donna Oswalt

All rights reserved. Written permission must be secured from the publisher to use or reproduce any part of this book, except for brief quotations in critical reviews or articles.

Printed in the United States of America

13   12   11   10   09   1   2   3   4   5

Library of Congress Control Number: 2009932689

ISBN: 978-1-57736-419-1

Cover and page design by LeAnna Massingille

Unless otherwise noted, all Scripture is taken from The Message. Copyright © by Eugene H. Peterson 1993, 1994, 1995, 1996, 2000, 2001, 2002. Used by permission of NavPress Publishing Group.

Scripture quotations marked NASB are taken from the New American Standard Bible®. Copyright © 1960, 1962, 1968, 1971, 1972, 1973, 1975, 1977, 1995 by The Lockman Foundation. Used by permission.

Scripture quotations marked NRSV are taken from the Holy Bible: New Revised Standard Version/Division of Christian Education of the National Council of Churches of Christ in the United States of America.—Nashville: Thomas Nelson Publishers, © 1989. Used by permission. All rights reserved.

Scripture quotations marked TLB or The Living Bible are taken from The Living Bible [computer file]/Kenneth N. Taylor.—electronic ed.—Wheaton: Tyndale House, 1997,c1971 by Tyndale House Publishers, Inc. Used by permission. All rights reserved.

Scripture quotations marked NIV are taken from HOLY BIBLE, NEW INTERNATIONAL VERSION®. Copyright © 1973, 1978, 1984 by International Bible Society. Used by permission of Zondervan Publishing House.

Scripture quotations marked NJB are taken from The New Jerusalem Bible, standard edition. © 1999 by Doubleday. All rights reserved.

Scripture quotations marked NLT are taken from the Holy Bible, New Living Translation, copyright 1996, 2004. Used by permission of Tyndale House Publishers, Inc., Wheaton, Illinois 60189. All rights reserved.

Scripture quotations marked NCV are taken from The Holy Bible, New Century Version, copyright © 1987, 1988, 1991 by Word Publishing, a division of Thomas Nelson, Inc. Used by permission.

PROVIDENCE HOUSE PUBLISHERS
238 Seaboard Lane • Franklin, Tennessee 37067
www.providencehouse.com
800-321-5692

To God-of-the-Angel-Armies—
Your promises give me life, and
I delight in being Yours.

To my husband, Ken, and our daughters,
Jennifer and Allison—Your generous love and
laughter embrace my life beyond words.

To my prayer partner and God-chosen friend,
Sharon Head—Your steady encouragement
champions and humbles my soul.

Contents

Preface	ix
Shrove Tuesday: *Prepare the Heart*	3
Ash Wednesday: *Mark of a Sinner*	5
Thursday: *Illusion and Temptation*	7
Friday: *Empty and Exposed*	9
Saturday: *Busy and Broken*	11
First Sunday in Lent: *Move into the Center*	13
Monday: *Sin Disguised*	15
Tuesday: *Grace Can*	17
Wednesday: *Hurried Harvest*	19
Thursday: *Specific Instructions*	21
Friday: *Rescue Call*	23
Saturday: *Steady Light*	25
Second Sunday in Lent: *Power and Possibility*	27
Monday: *Everlasting and Unfailing*	29
Tuesday: *Hope's Promises*	31
Wednesday: *Obedient Servant*	33
Thursday: *Into the Light*	35
Friday: *Telling the Story*	37
Saturday: *Spirit Divine*	39
Third Sunday in Lent: *Mystery and Majesty*	41
Monday: *Wide Open*	43
Tuesday: *Moments in the Middle*	45

Wednesday: *Unexpected Whispers*	47
Thursday: *Altar of Holiness*	49
Friday: *Perfector of Endurance*	51
Saturday: *See Jesus*	53
Fourth Sunday in Lent: *Real Love*	55
Monday: *Good Deeds*	57
Tuesday: *Splendor of His Love*	59
Wednesday: *Response to Living Hope*	61
Thursday: *A Living Letter*	63
Friday: *How Christ Loves*	65
Saturday: *Turning Point*	67
Fifth Sunday in Lent: *Living Holiness*	69
Monday: *Refined Design*	71
Tuesday: *More than Enough*	73
Wednesday: *Everlasting Testimony*	75
Thursday: *Everything and All*	77
Friday: *Fruitful Harvest*	79
Saturday: *In His Hand*	81
Palm Sunday: *Glorious Hope*	83
Monday: *Pierced Righteousness*	85
Tuesday: *Perfect Lamb*	87
Wednesday: *Betrayed*	90
Maundy Thursday: *Perfect Love Intercedes*	92
Good Friday: *Amazing Love*	94
Saturday: *Rest and Restoration*	96
Easter Sunday: *Kindled Soul, Holy Fire*	99
ABOUT THE AUTHOR	102

Preface

Oswald Chambers, in *My Utmost for His Highest*, wrote:

> God takes us beyond our own aspirations and ideas for our lives, and molds and shapes us for His purpose . . .

This book is a collection of devotions and prayers designed for the Lenten season. When we recognize our greatest needs in the shadow of the cross, we find God's greatest gift. During this season of hope, read and meditate on God's extravagant love, the giving of grace through His Son, Jesus Christ. Then embrace the fire that His presence kindles within your soul.

> So here's what I want you to do, God helping you: Take your everyday, ordinary life—your sleeping, eating, going-to-work, and walking-around life—and place it before God as an offering. Embracing what God does for you is the best thing you can do for him.
>
> —**Romans 12:1**

Trusting in Him,
Donna Oswalt

Kindled Soul Holy Fire

Shrove Tuesday
Prepare the Heart

> Whatever you have said in the dark will be heard in the light, and what you have whispered behind closed doors will be shouted from the housetops for all to hear! . . . I tell you the truth, everyone who acknowledges me publicly here on earth, the Son of Man will also acknowledge in the presence of God's angels.
>
> **Luke 12:3, 8 (NLT)**

Today is Shrove Tuesday. To my Protestant ears, this is a foreign label. I have learned it is another way of saying *Mardi Gras*, or Fat Tuesday. Shrove derives its meaning, "to repent," from Old English and refers to a day of spiritual preparation for Lent, which begins tomorrow with Ash Wednesday.

This day I have meditated on Luke 12. Jesus, speaking before crowds of thousands, warns his disciples about the Pharisees and "the way they pretend to be good when they aren't" (v. 1, TLB).

As the season of Hope begins tomorrow, my soul longs to hear His voice, know His will, understand His love, and experience His grace. Like the Pharisees, I too can become consumed with myself, thinking of my needs as more important. In the days of this Lenten season, I long to prepare my heart for the celebration of His Glory!

Holy Father:

Arrogance and pride do not belong only to the Pharisees; they are my markers of sin. Forgive me when I bring my agenda to Your altar, when I seek my plans above Your promises. You are the Messiah, my Savior and Lord. I am humbled by Your generous love and honored by Your grace-full invitation—to know You as Friend! With a repentant heart—Amen!

PERSONAL REFLECTIONS

ASH WEDNESDAY

Mark of a Sinner

> . . . [Jesus] led them up a high mountain. His appearance changed from the inside out, right before their eyes. Sunlight poured from his face. His clothes were filled with light . . . a light-radiant cloud enveloped them, and sounding from deep in the cloud a voice: "This is my Son, marked by my love, focus of my delight. Listen to him."
>
> Matthew 17:1b–2, 5

Ash Wednesday reminds the soul to listen with a penitent heart. This day is the seventh Wednesday before Easter Sunday and marks the first day of the Lenten season, a time of reflection. While this time of somber remembrance has not been common in many mainline Protestant churches, Ash Wednesday services are increasing. People seem to be seeking more meaning in their faith, a greater understanding of Christianity.

Ashes, made by burning the palms from last year's Palm Sunday, become the mark of a sinner. The dictionary defines penitence as "remorse for past conduct, to regret sinning, contrition." This is required for our salvation, to have a contrite and repentant heart, but our humility before the Lord must be daily. In the busyness of life, we forget this. In the chaos of life, we try to control. In the routine of life, we get lazy. In the disappointments of life, we despair. The heart becomes fragmented, humility becomes pride, peace becomes anxiety, success becomes arrogance, inconvenience becomes frustration. We are marked by our thoughts and actions, our intentions and omissions.

Jesus, Delight of the Holy Father:

I kneel before You with a contrite heart, regretting my sins. Even if I confess my sins every moment, I remain a sinner, unable to redeem my life. Humility of heart gets trampled in the everyday. This sinner likes to be in control, find the perfect solution, grasp the best idea. Forgive my foolish attempts to take Your job. With Your amazing grace, I have been changed from the inside out. Only, I forget this gift, this undeserved and unmerited favor You freely give. Jesus, I desire to honor You, to live so that others may know I have been marked by Your love! Remembering the cost of grace, Amen!

PERSONAL REFLECTIONS

THURSDAY

Illusion and Temptation

> Now Jesus, full of the Holy Spirit, left the Jordan and was led by the Spirit into the wild. For forty wilderness days and nights he was tested by the Devil. . . . That completed the testing. The Devil retreated temporarily, lying in wait for another opportunity.
>
> Luke 4:1–2, 13

Even as the Holy Spirit guided Jesus, the devil lurked, waiting and plotting to tempt the Son of God. Three times the devil tried to tempt Jesus to sin. Each time, Jesus quoted from Scripture, the Word, giving support for His refusal to follow the evil one's offers to satisfy hunger, to give the illusion of power, to test God. As I read these verses, I realized that with each reply Jesus used the Bible as His resource for answers, as His responses of truth.

In the first verse of John's Gospel we read:

> In the beginning was the Word, and the Word was with God, and the Word was God. . . . The Word became flesh and made his dwelling among us. We have seen his glory, the glory of the One and Only, who came from the Father, full of grace and truth.
>
> —John 1:1, 14 (NIV)

We must seek answers and find truth in the Word, the Holy Scriptures, our earthly resource. God reveals Himself through the Word. Jesus, who taught us by example, is the Living Word.

The illusions of the world that lure us into thinking we know a better way masquerade as knowledge. Darkness pervades where there is no light. The words that must not be overlooked are the ones that often try to hide behind truth. "The Devil retreated" suggests defeat. However, we must not forget that the evil one is always "lying in wait for another opportunity."

El Elyon, the Lord Most High:

The world lures me with its false security, its partial truths, its hidden agendas. Forgive me when I stumble, tempted and tossed. It is pride that prods my mind with a sense of control in the presence of chaos. Teach me how to recognize evil's lies, its cunning way, its deceptive touch.

Jesus spoke the Word in response to temptation, in defense of Truth. Fill me with the Living Word, a grace that is beyond my understanding. Guard my heart; alert my mind to evil's ever-present threat. Let the Word be my response when darkness seizes my moments of weakness, when lies shout louder. Holy Spirit, whisper to my yearning soul. I am listening. I am looking for Your glory, full of grace and truth. Amen.

❧ PERSONAL REFLECTIONS ☙

FRIDAY

Empty and Exposed

> But He gives a greater grace. Therefore it says, "GOD IS OPPOSED TO THE PROUD, BUT GIVES GRACE TO THE HUMBLE."
>
> James 4:6 (NASB)

*E*verywhere I look, winter's trees stand bare, all their branches exposed, and even the smallest branches can be seen. Their empty and barren appearance can be misleading. After all, dead trees look this way for a long time before decay fractures them. These trees, however, are not dead, just resting. This dormant time prepares them for new beginnings, new growth.

In this season of reflection, I stand bare and exposed at His altar, down to my smallest flaws. For one to surrender to examination, all must be placed on the altar: all disappointment, failure, and regret; all dreams, successes, and blessings. My intentions must be revealed, my desires probed. My soul is naked before the Most High, for He searches me and knows my every thought and motive. He seeks a contrite heart, a repentant heart. "He gives a greater grace."

> God hasn't invited us into a disorderly, unkempt life but into something holy and beautiful—as beautiful on the inside as the outside.
>
> —1 Thessalonians 4:7

When the Creator dresses the trees in beautiful blossoms and tender green leaves, the season of renewal will give glory to His provision. I long to be made new.

Jehovah-Jireh, the Lord our Provider:

I come before You, empty of all the trappings that attempt to hide my sins. On my knees at the altar I surrender my selfishness, my loneliness, my self-serving interests. I place my disappointments at Your feet, my tears confessing wordless hurt and sadness and grief. I fail to hear Your voice, fail to choose Your way. When everything favors my desires and circumstances are sweet, I hear the world's applause. Forgive me. I abandon my barren efforts and seek Your tender renewal. Lord, order my mind with worthy thoughts, holy and true. Dress my heart with new blossoms, beautiful for You. Clothe my soul with greater grace. Amen.

PERSONAL REFLECTIONS

SATURDAY

Busy and Broken

> But Jesus Himself would **often** slip away to the wilderness and pray.
>
> Luke 5:16 (NASB, **emphasis added**)

Our calendars only begin to tell the story of our busyness. Cell phones distract us. Computers betray us. Commitments divide us. We try to be all things to everyone, doing everything all the time. "Collect, collate, and conquer" becomes our unspoken mantra. The soul runs near empty.

I know there are necessary duties, essential tasks, and recurrent chores. Many worthy endeavors request our time, need our attention, demand our efforts. In my honest moments, I wonder how many does the Father choose, which ones bring Him glory, where does His plan lead? The only way to hear these answers is to spend time in prayer, away from the crowds.

Prayer connects us to God. Jesus would frequently withdraw to a secluded place and pray, teaching His disciples by example. We must imitate Jesus, our hearts calling to the Father. Praying with praises and confessions, seeking with intention and perseverance, and listening with contrition and patience, we must come to the altar to be alone with God.

Holy Father:

Glimpses of Your glory escape me because I hurry past or rush between or skip ahead. Your best moments are hidden in my eagerness, my enthusiasm, my certainty. Forgive the careless and egocentric attitudes that clog my days and blind my heart to the unmeasured blessings.

In the silence of the early morning, let me linger in Your presence, a fragrance fresh and sweet. In the darkness of the late night, let me sit with You, with wisdom strong and true. In the solitude of an afternoon walk or in the stillness as children lie sleeping, I desire to rest with You, a shelter safe and warm. Tell me where to go and what to choose. Help me know how and when and if. Oh, Father, as I wait, give me patience to be still long enough to listen, to be quiet long enough to hear Your whispers of love. Amen.

PERSONAL REFLECTIONS

First Sunday in Lent
Move into the Center

> He must become greater and greater, and I must become less and less.
>
> John 3:30 (NLT)

When I ponder the greatness of God, my thoughts often turn to creation. While not the popular idea among some scientific minds, I believe God is the Creator. As I look for Him in creation, I find His fingerprints everywhere, from the crisp, morning air to the brilliant stars that decorate the night sky and infinite places in between. God is in the details of creation, the details of our circumstances, the details of our curiosities. He is a God of power and wonder.

> He must increase, but I must decrease.
>
> —John 3:30 (NASB)

When I reflect on my finite journey, I realize the details life creates are miniscule compared to the formation of the earth. While I am preoccupied with my family, commitments, or friends, God remains faithful. As I schedule the appointments, plan the trips, and complete the forms, God waits for me. I give too much importance to the routine tasks and not enough attention to the Creator of time, the Creator of purpose, the Creator of me. He is a God of faithfulness and patience.

> This is the assigned moment for him to move into the center, while I slip off to the sidelines.
>
> —John 3:30

When examining my heart, I realize my desires often take precedence over His. While I believe Jesus is my Savior, my actions leave a different impression. As His presence draws me near, I struggle to hear, pray, and respond. His compassions are endless, His mercies fresh and new every day. In these moments, I put myself away and enter a time of seeking, a time of listening, a time of nourishment. He is a God of grace and love.

Creator, Giver of all good things,

You are larger than my imagination and grander than my dreams, greater than my needs. Your goodness surrounds me, bathing me in light and love. Forgive me when I ignore You and give You only the leftover places in my life. The beauty of Your world challenges my mind to higher thoughts and deeper study. The tenderness of Your patience reminds my heart to listen more and want less. The compassion of Your forgiveness refreshes my soul in ways that I cannot explain. You are bountiful grace and enduring love.

Help me know You, really know You. Teach me to love like You love, forgive like You forgive, and listen like You listen. Strengthen me with Your presence. I long to be less so You can be more. Thank You for loving me beyond boundaries! Amen.

PERSONAL REFLECTIONS

Monday

Sin Disguised

> For we naturally love to do evil things that are just the opposite from the things that the Holy Spirit tells us to do; and the good things we want to do when the Spirit has his way with us are just the opposite of our natural desires. These two forces within us are constantly fighting each other to win control over us, and our wishes are never free from their pressures.
>
> **Galatians 5:17 (TLB)**

The root of our sinful nature corrupts our best intentions. When evil's list of influences is posted, we argue our innocence in most of the categories. This somehow gives us a feeling of superiority over those who commit the "bigger" sins like murder and adultery and stealing. We slyly smile and agree that we are guilty of the "lesser" sins like envy or gossip or anger. But God does not categorize sin.

Because we are fallen creatures, our actions often reflect impurity. We struggle with our motives, our priorities, our personal investments. Our image in the community struggles with our Christian witness. While our generosity in financial giving seeks recognition, our shallow faith hides. Pride and selfishness battle for first place while dissatisfaction and criticism beg for attention. Satan always disguises sin in attractive packages.

God of mercy and compassion:

How difficult to come before You and confess my sins. How easy to ignore them, to pretend that I have it all together. How foolish I am, for You already know the intentions of my heart, the thoughts of my mind, the emptiness of my soul. Forgive me when I try to justify my sin in the name of doing for others. Forgive me when I seek recognition for Your gifts. Forgive me when I do not come to You for truth and boldness and encouragement, when I try to find these in the world.

Evil teases and tempts and tricks me into thinking I know what is good and right. The world applauds my gestures. But Jesus, I am wrong. I desire to take the easy way, the shorter path, the better road. But You go with me through difficult times, along narrow trails and into refining fires. The world laughs at me; evil taunts me and calls me weak. In the conflict of good and evil, through the chaos of right and wrong, I hear a song from my childhood . . . *Jesus loves me this I know; for the Bible tells me so. Little ones to Him belong; they are weak, but He is strong.*

Yes, Jesus, I am weak, but I know You are strong, strong enough to carry me until I can stand again. You are stronger than anything in this world. Hold me, Jesus. Help me, Jesus. Heal me, Jesus. Amen.

PERSONAL REFLECTIONS

TUESDAY

Grace Can

> Those who belong to Christ have nailed their natural evil desires to his cross and crucified them there.
> **Galatians 5:24 (TLB)**

Sandwiched between the fruits of the Spirit (verses 22–23) and following the Holy Spirit's leading (verse 25) is the meat! God cannot produce fruit in us like love, joy, peace, patience, kindness, goodness, faithfulness, gentleness, and self-control unless we belong to Christ. In confession of our natural evil desires, we admit that we do not have control, cannot buy grace, will not conquer death. Jesus allowed our sins to be nailed to cross and crucified there.

If we belong to Christ, the Holy Spirit guides our lives. To follow the Holy Spirit's leading requires a change of focus. No longer can we look to ourselves for answers, to others for satisfaction, and to the world for outcomes. This new relationship we have with Jesus is complete, full, and perfect. His grace is more than enough. And still, He gives us more—life everlasting. Jesus wore the sins of us all, with wounds and thorns and nails. In his book *Captured by Grace*, David Jeremiah calls this "grace that is too marvelous for words."[1]

Jesus:

This holy fruit You harvest is what I want. This relationship that completes me, fills me, and perfects me is what I desire. This grace that exceeds words is what I need. Choose me.

There are busy days when I forget You. There are glory-moments when I take credit for my success. There are stressful times when I blame You for my consequences. Forgive me.

Such perfect love I did not know before nailing my sins to the cross through You. Such soul-satisfaction I did not find before belonging to You. Such heart-contentment I did not have before following You.

I am chosen! I am forgiven! I am loved! Amen.

PERSONAL REFLECTIONS

---

1. David Jeremiah, *Captured by Grace: No One Is Beyond the Reach of a Loving God* (Nashville: Integrity Publishers, 2006), n.p.

Wednesday
Hurried Harvest

> What a person plants, he will harvest. The person who plants selfishness, ignoring the needs of others—ignoring God!—harvests a crop of weeds. All he'll have to show for his life is weeds! But the one who plants in response to God, letting God's Spirit do the growth work in him, harvests a crop of real life, eternal life.
>
> **Galatians 6:7b-8**

We live in a world that is always on fast forward. Sometimes it seems we are always running behind schedule, hurrying between errands, falling into impatience. Much of the time, we see only the task before us. In our hurried living, we often ignore God. While you might disagree, defending your position with those moments of prayer or quickly read daily devotionals, it would be worthy to ask yourself, "When was the last time I noticed God?"

Did you see Him in the yellow daffodils? Did you feel Him in the warmth of the sunshine? Did you notice Him in the elderly lady at the grocery store? Did you hear Him in the children's laughter? Did you touch Him when you held the hand of your hurting friend? Did you smell Him in the sweet fragrance of spring's hyacinths? In our busyness we ignore God, but He never forgets us, always reaching for our hand

and loving us without condition. God says as He waits, "Let's get together more often! I miss you!"

Lord of the Harvest:

The seeds of selfishness and hurriedness do not grow crops of goodness and graciousness. The seeds of impatience and frustration do not grow crops of kindness and joy. The seeds of worry and anger do not grow crops of peace and contentment. My harvest is full of weeds.

You harvest crops planted with the Holy Spirit. You grow seeds of righteousness into harvests of blessings. You are the Master Gardener, holy and good. I long to spend time with You; I yearn to find Your presence in the ordinary moments. Deep inside, beyond the chaos, I hear You calling to me. My soul sings its song of weariness and confesses, I miss You, too! Amen.

PERSONAL REFLECTIONS

THURSDAY
Specific Instructions

> The word of GOD came to Solomon saying, "About this Temple you are building—what's important is that you *live* the way I've set out for you and *do* what I tell you, following my instructions carefully and obediently. Then I'll complete in you the promise I made to David your father. I'll personally take up my residence among the Israelites—I won't desert my people Israel."
>
> 1 Kings 6:11–13

Four years into his reign, Solomon, the wisest king of Israel's history, was tasked with building the Temple in Jerusalem. It would take seven years to complete, following very specific details given by God. Although Solomon's achievements brought honor to the nation of Israel and to God, the worship of idols caused the people to abandon God for their own personal desires. God wanted to live within their hearts, not be confined to the Temple.

While these ancient words were given to Solomon regarding the specifics for building the Temple in Jerusalem, there are lessons for us today. As God is building His Temple within us, we must live within God's parameters and do what God tells us. Our lives must reflect Him in all that we do; our obedience to Him is key. God's promise to us is Jesus. Through the Holy Spirit, God resides in us; we become the Temple of the Living God.

God—the Master Architect:

Your promises to me are made through a New Covenant—Jesus Christ. You have personally taken up residence in my soul through the Holy Spirit. This Temple knows You are the foundation and have specific instructions for me—for my mind, heart, and soul. To follow Your plan carefully and obediently is my greatest desire. So, as You tell me how to live and what to do, I promise to listen for Your voice, obey Your leading, and live by Your love. And when my human heart forgets Your words, remind me. For I know Your mercy is infinitely deep; Your faithfulness is neverending. You will not let me go! Amen.

PERSONAL REFLECTIONS

Friday
Rescue Call

You who sit down in the High God's presence,
   spend the night in Shaddai's shadow,
Say this: "God, you're my refuge.
   I trust in you and I'm safe!"
That's right—he rescues you from hidden traps,
   shields you from deadly hazards.
His huge outstretched arms protect you—
   under them you're perfectly safe;
   his arms fend off all harm.
Fear nothing—not wild wolves in the night,
   not flying arrows in the day.
Not disease that prowls through the darkness,
   not disaster that erupts at high noon.
Even though others succumb all around,
   drop like flies right and left,
   no harm will even graze you.
You'll stand untouched, watch it all from a distance,
   watch the wicked turn into corpses.
Yes, because GOD's your refuge,
   the High God your very own home,
Evil can't get close to you,
   harm can't get through the door.
He ordered His angels
   to guard you wherever you go.
If you stumble, they'll catch you;
   their job is to keep you from falling.

> You'll walk unharmed among among lions and snakes,
>> and kick young lions and serpents from the path.
> "If you hold on to me for dear life," says GOD,
>> "I'll get you out of any trouble.
> I'll give you the best of care
>> if you'll only get to know and trust me.
> Call me and I'll answer, be at your side in bad times;
>> I'll rescue you, then throw you a party.
> I'll give you a long life,
>> give you a long drink of salvation!"
>
> **Psalm 91**

El Shaddai, God All-Sufficient:

With Your presence, providence, provision, and protection, be my shelter and my rest! Your angels gather near, watching over me. Whether evil lurks in the darkness or shouts boldly in the daylight, You are my rescue! When all seems uncertain and the way unclear, I place my trust in You. I call to You. And You answer me, calling me by name. Amen.

PERSONAL REFLECTIONS

Saturday

Steady Light

> Whatever is good and perfect comes down to us from God our Father, who created all the lights in the heavens. He never changes or casts a shifting shadow. He chose to give birth to us by giving us his true word. And we, out of all creation, became his prized possession.
>
> **James 1:17–18 (NLT)**

Tonight there was a total lunar eclipse, the first one in three years. While an uncommon event, as the moon is usually above or below the earth's orbit, this occurs when the earth passes between the sun and the moon. Because the sunlight is refracted, the earth's shadow on the moon appears to be crimson red in color. While His heavenly lights change orbits and cast shifting shadows, God never changes.

As I watched the eclipse tonight, I marveled at the Creator and His magnificent creation. Everything good comes from God. Because of His goodness, He chose to make us His own children by giving us His true word. What mystery and majesty to think that God chooses us to be His children. And we, out of all creation, became His prized possession.

Father of Lights:

The heavenly lights, the sun and moon and stars, shout glory! Father, You are Light! These magnificent creations change with the seasons! Orbits and rotations, gravity and eclipses alter appearances. Father, You never change. You are the Constant Force.

Out of Your goodness, You choose us! We can call, "Father! Abba!" Of all Your amazing creations, we are Your favorite! I am humbled by such divine design. While all around me is shifting, the world full of shadows, You remain a steady light. You are perfect love! Amen.

PERSONAL REFLECTIONS

Second Sunday in Lent
Power and Possibility

> O Sovereign LORD! You made the heavens and earth by your strong hand and powerful arm. Nothing is too hard for you!
>
> **Jeremiah 32:17 (NLT)**

The Lord told Jeremiah to purchase a field just outside Jerusalem even though the land had been captured by the Babylonians, Israel's enemy. Although it seemed like an unwise investment, Jeremiah followed the Lord's message, an act of faith in God's promises to Israel. Afterward, Jeremiah offered a prayer acknowledging God's power over impossibility. He prayed, "Nothing is too hard for You!"

Spoken to Jeremiah:

> This is what the LORD says—the LORD who made the earth, who formed and established it, whose name is the Lord: Ask me and I will tell you remarkable secrets you do not know about things to come.
>
> —Jer. 33:2–3 (NLT)

God gave Jeremiah assurance that Israel will one day have peace and prosperity. The capture of Jerusalem did not change God's ultimate plan; nothing changes God's purposes. God alone is Creator and Judge and Redeemer. His faithful love desires that we come to His altar and ask. We must pray, "Nothing is too hard for You!"

Jehovah-Elohim, the Eternal Creator:

Infinite in power, measureless in love, You are my blessed assurance. I fall to my knees before the Maker of all. I am humbled by the Love Most High. Trusting in Your promises demands faith in the impossible. My heart finds itself wordless in the presence of holiness. In awe and wonder, my soul whispers, "Nothing is too hard for You!" Amen.

❧ PERSONAL REFLECTIONS ☙

MONDAY

Everlasting and Unfailing

> ". . . I will care for the survivors as they travel through the wilderness. I will again come to give rest to the people of Israel." Long ago the LORD said to Israel: "I have loved you, my people, with an everlasting love. With unfailing love I have drawn you to myself."
> **Jeremiah 31:2–3 (NLT, 1996 version)**

Through the prophet Jeremiah, God sent messages of hope and restoration to Israel. He promised that one day Israel would return to their land, that Jerusalem would be rebuilt. God cared for them during the time in the wilderness, and after their release from Babylonian captivity, this promise was realized. The second message was one of hope. He promised everlasting love to His chosen people. He promised a final restoration in the Messiah.

Today, His messages of hope and restoration still speak to us. God's unfailing love draws us to Him. His promise of everlasting love is found in the Redeemer, the Word made flesh. Christ is our eternal hope. By faith in Christ, we are gathered into the family of God. His immutable love will hold us until the Messiah returns. Then, His promise of our final restoration will be fulfilled.

Adonai:

We struggle in our own wilderness of doubt and fear, or uncertainty and possibility, or loneliness and disappointment, or regret and despair. Sometimes we get lost; we get weary. But if we listen, there is a voice calling to us, "Come to Me, and I will give you rest." Lord, You are Hope.

When we hear Your words, "I have loved you with an everlasting love," our mouths are silenced. Such love cannot be fully understood. We feel Your presence and are drawn to Your unfailing love. In this holy solitude, the promise of mercy restores the soul. Lord, You are Eternal Hope. Amen.

PERSONAL REFLECTIONS

TUESDAY
Hope's Promises

> Keep me safe O God,
> for in you I take refuge.
> I said to the LORD, "You are my Lord;
> apart from you I have no good thing." ... LORD, you
> have assigned me my portion and my cup;
> you have made my lot secure.
> The boundary lines have fallen for me in pleasant places;
> surely I have a delightful inheritance.
>
> **Psalm 16:1–2, 5–6 (NIV)**

When the road seems long, we can always find refuge in God. He is our shelter in the storm and our anchor in the raging sea. Often we define ourselves by our circumstances, rather than by our relationship with God. The blessings that come our way can be overlooked when our focus shifts from God to the world. Despite experiences of difficulty and disappointment, God's goodness prevails.

John Newton, a slave trader who became a pastor, penned the words to one of Christianity's most famous hymns, "Amazing Grace." One verse is seldom found in today's hymnals:

> The Lord has promised good to me,
> His Word my hope secures;

> He will my Shield and Portion be,
> As long as life endures.

With God's promises of goodness and His Word, we can have hope in all circumstances. He protects and provides in all the ways we need. *The Message* translates Psalm 16:2 this way: "Without you, nothing makes sense." Even when the world creates chaos in our lives, God can always take our hearts to pleasant places. With Christ, we have a delightful inheritance.

Adonai:

You are Goodness in all times. Every good and perfect gift comes from You. The world shouts for our attention, distracts and demeans us, but You lift us up, give us hope, shield our hearts, and protect our future.

You take us to the high places of blessing (Eph. 1:3), confirming our inheritance. You are our Shield and Portion. You are Everlasting Life. Without You, nothing makes sense. Amen.

◈ PERSONAL REFLECTIONS ◈

Wednesday

Obedient Servant

> [The angel said to Mary:] for nothing is impossible to God. Mary said, "You see before you the Lord's servant, let it happen to me as you have said." . . .
>
> **Luke 1:37–38 (NJB)**

Am I eager to be used by God? Is my heart open to God's whispers? Are His messengers bringing me instructions? What happens when I doubt His plan? Do I consider the cost of following Him? Will I still choose to be obedient to Him? The implications for Mary were great, yet she was a willing servant. Am I?

There are times when I listen intently for the Gentle Shepherd, following His commands. Other times the world distracts me with ridicule, dividing my loyalties. The Word speaks His truth to my heart, and doubts disappear. Then darkness calls with its words of partial truths and lures my thoughts. I desire to listen for the Love Most High and long to be His obedient servant. Will I?

Love Most High:

You have come in the form of Perfect Love to rescue me, imperfect in every way. You seek me despite my flaws, offering more than forgiveness. You offer me eternal hope!

And me? I whine about the places You choose for me to serve and the people who do not meet my needs and the possibility of failure or rejection.

My soul falls to its knees before You, listening for the divine whispers of the Holy Spirit. Forgive my weakness and selfishness and doubt. Rescue me from the world's opinions. I do believe nothing is impossible to God and long to be Your obedient servant. So be it!

PERSONAL REFLECTIONS

THURSDAY

Into the Light

> I will be glad and rejoice in your unfailing love, for you have seen my troubles, and you care about the anguish of my soul.
>
> **Psalm 31:7 (NLT)**

We are not promised a life without difficulty, and so sometimes come to the conclusion that anguish is inevitable, disappointment captures joy, and circumstances create division. So, how do we identify the problem? When we find ourselves standing in a shadow, there must be light somewhere. The shadow-maker can always be found between the shadow and the light. Evil's victory is hurt and deception and doubt; he is the joy-stealer!

When the world comes between us and the Light, we lose our way. Living in the shadow keeps the heart from understanding the truth. The Light reveals the truth and identifies the problem. God's unfailing love calls to us, giving us faith to step out of the shadow and into the light. God's glory is love and truth and light; He is Joy!

Lord, holy and true:

I stand in the shadow and weep, for darkness surrounds me. Slander and lies come from all directions like arrows from a skilled marksman. I call to You. Help me know the truth.

In the distance I see the Light. You call to me, "My child, I love you!" You reach for me and take my hand, gently leading me from the shadow-maker. In faith, I step into the Light and am made new.

Your holy presence warms my soul. Your unfailing love delights my soul. Your unmeasured grace cleanses my soul. I am made complete in You. Amen.

❧ PERSONAL REFLECTIONS ☙

FRIDAY

Telling the Story

> As [Jesus] was getting into the boat, the man who had been demon-possessed was imploring Him that he might accompany Him. And He did not let him, but He said to him, "Go home to your people and report to them what great things the Lord has done for you, and how He had mercy on you." And he went away and began to proclaim in Decapolis what great things Jesus had done for him; and everyone was amazed.
>
> Mark 5:18–20 (NASB)

The demon-possessed man was an outcast, wild and irrational. The community feared him. Jesus healed this man, but his change was so remarkable that the community did not know how to respond. The man wanted to go with Jesus, but He told the man to go home and "Tell them your story."

We carry deep wounds; sometimes they are Legion. In the silences, we visit these caves of painful words and hurtful acts, trying to understand the injustices. In our fear, we hide or attack, withdraw or fight, become arrogant or revengeful. We get lost in the illusions created by pain.

Our wounds can affect the way others perceive us. Sometimes we let our wounds control our lives. Often we hide behind our wounds, fearful of what they can teach us about ourselves. When Jesus heals our wounds, we struggle to express the deep emotions of gratitude, compassion, and love. Jesus responds, "Tell them your story."

Jesus, Healer of my soul:

Jesus, come and heal my wounds. Come and cleanse my heart, nourish my joy, renew my hope. You are the Healer, the Great Physician, who makes all things new. Your mercies soothe the deepest ache, the longest pain, the oldest scar. Encourage me with Your compassion, strengthen me through Your Word, hold me in Your arms.

How do I say thank you for perfect love and amazing grace? How many songs of praise can the heart sing? Jesus, I will tell my story—how You love without condition, touch the deepest wounds, heal with holy intention. I will tell my story of redemption. I will tell them about You! Amen.

PERSONAL REFLECTIONS

SATURDAY

Spirit Divine

> You know well enough how the wind blows this way and that. You hear it rustling through the trees, but you have no idea where it comes from or where it's headed next. That's the way it is with everyone "born from above" by the wind of God, the Spirit of God.
> **John 3:8b**

Holy Wind

A mighty gust, some gentle breezes,
Either blows wherever it pleases.
In silence passing, roaring through,
Hidden still, this Wind chooses you,

From south to north or west to east,
From weak to strong or more to least,
Invisible, with power to
Break and mend, this Wind comes to you.

Quietly with intense yearning,
The Wind flames a fire burning
Within the soul, consuming dross
That calls repentance to the cross.

From south to north or west to east,
From weak to strong or more to least,
This Perfect Love endures each nail
Which reconciles and rends the veil.

Infinitely bolder than deep,
Broader than wide, higher than steep,
Holy Wind, hold each empty place,
Mend my soul with marvelous grace.

Spirit of God:
Despite my sin—resume the call—define my heart!
Delight my mind—assume my sin—design my life!
Ignite the fire—consume the dross—refine my soul!
Invisible and Indescribable and Invincible! Take me now!
—Amen!

PERSONAL REFLECTIONS

Third Sunday in Lent
Mystery and Majesty

> "For my thoughts are not your thoughts, neither are your ways my ways," declares the LORD. "As the heavens are higher than the earth, so are my ways higher than your ways and my thoughts higher than your thoughts. As the rain and the snow come down from heaven, and do not return to it without watering the earth and making it bud and flourish, so that it yields seed for the sower and bread for the eater, so is my word that goes out from my mouth: It will not return to me empty, but will accomplish what I desire and achieve the purpose for which I sent it. You will go out in joy and be led forth in peace; the mountains and hills will burst into song before you, and all the trees of the field will clap their hands."
>
> **Isaiah 55:8–12 (NIV)**

Thoughts of His mystery and majesty lay without equity beside thoughts of His willingness and wounds. The contrast of His glory and His sacrifice boldly confronts my heart. Indescribable! God exceeds my imagination. He invites each of us to come to the Living Water so that our thirst can be quenched. He is the Bread of heaven that can feed every soul. He gives us the Living Word to accomplish His purposes. The Great Provider meets all needs.

This is the season of new beginnings. Just as the Scriptures say, the mountains and hills will burst into song before you, and all the trees of the field will clap their hands, and spring arrives. Blossoms and new leaves reveal His glory and shout praises to their Maker. My heart delights in such majesty, and my soul is renewed with hope.

Jehovah-Jireh:

God of our provision, You have thought of everything, considered every need of every creation. I am moved to tears at the splendor of Your beauty. You are everywhere this splendid day—in blooming trees and singing birds, in fragrant blossoms and colors of every shade. I find You in the gentle breeze and the touch of human hands, in the smiles and tears and hurts and joys of those You bring my way.

Your thoughts and ways are greater than I can understand. The when's and how's and where's and why's bind me. I do not understand pain for its purpose, loss for its gain, or grief for its joy. I do not know the reason the eagle soars on Your wind and never asks how or why it must fly. These mysteries transcend my finite mind. And yet, I am sure of how to quench my thirst and feed my soul. My prayers rise to unknown heights that I cannot reach as I find a love that is deeper than deep. Living Water, I thirst for more. Living Word, I hunger for more. Living God, be my Shalom. Amen.

PERSONAL REFLECTIONS

MONDAY

Wide Open

> For whatever God says to us is full of living power: it is sharper than the sharpest dagger, cutting swiftly and deep into our innermost thoughts and desires with all their parts, exposing us for what we really are. He knows about everyone, everywhere. Everything about us is bare and wide open to the all-seeing eyes of our living God; nothing can be hidden from him to whom we must explain all that we have done.
>
> **Hebrews 4:12–13 (TLB)**

The Holy Scriptures speak to us with living power because God's Word is alive. He knows the intentions of our hearts, which we often disguise with good actions, appropriate words, and helpful gestures. We are like open books to the all-seeing eyes of our living God and will one day be face to face with our Maker, responding to all that we have done. We will stand naked before the Holy One, exposed for what we really are.

Sovereign God:

You are omniscient, knowing all. You knew me before the foundations of the earth, knew my unformed body in the womb. You know my hopes and dreams, my sorrows and frustrations, my anxieties and disappointments. There is nothing about me that You do not know. Yes, Lord, that means You know all my thoughts and all my motivations.

You know the places in my heart that harbor darkness and the insides of my soul that rest under the wings of Your grace. You know the plans You have for me, plans for good, to give me a future and a hope (Jer. 29:11).

I fall to my knees, realizing that I do not always trust Your plans or recognize Your appointed times. Sometimes I try to tell You what is best for me. I do not listen for Your voice, do not feel Your presence. When darkness tempts me, I falter. Yet, Your Word remains ever true. You know me inside and out and love me still. You have plans for my future, good plans, plans filled with hope. Lord, forgive my restless impatience, my prideful thinking, my spiritual deafness. You alone are Maker and Redeemer. You are El Elyon, the Lord Most High. Amen.

❦ PERSONAL REFLECTIONS ❦

Tuesday
Moments in the Middle

> Be still, and know that I am God!
>
> Psalm 46:10a (NLT)

The world does not want silence and fills us with noise. Finding time to be with God can be challenge enough, but silence too? Then, when the moments of silence appear, thoughts dance inside the quiet—not thoughts of God, but of obligations, tasks, jobs, relationships, expectations, and the like. True silence comes in the middle of a crowd, between the red light and the green light, after dropping the children at school and before work, in the first moments after waking and in the last moments before sleeping.

Finding large portions of uninterrupted silence, time to be completely alone with the Father, must seem like dessert; an extra delight! It is unlikely that many of us always get dessert, sometimes we skip it. This is how our quiet time with God often goes. However, it is rare that we miss the main course. Being silent with God should be more like the main course, the essential nourishment. Finding time to hear His voice, witness His majesty, and delight in His presence demands that we give our attention to the moments in the middle of the minutes. We must find true silence.

Lord Almighty:

You alone are God. You are holy and good. Your presence can be felt in the silence. I wrestle with the world's noise as it always wants to distract me, numb my senses, hide Your voice. Teach me to find the silence that rests within my soul. Teach me to find You.

When the day begins and when it ends, I can come to Your altar. In the middle of hurry and at the beginning of busy, I can listen for Your Word. As the hectic pace escalates and the chaos declines, I can hear Your whispers. You are faithful and patient with me. True Silence, I long to know You are near. Amen.

PERSONAL REFLECTIONS

Wednesday
Unexpected Whispers

> But blessed are those who trust in the LORD and have made the LORD their hope and confidence. They are like trees planted along a riverbank, with roots that reach deep into the water. Such trees are not bothered by the heat or worried by long months of drought. Their leaves stay green, and they never stop producing fruit.
>
> **Jeremiah 17:7–8 (NLT)**

Blessings continually come to Christians, but the problem lies in not taking time to consider our blessings. How frequently we notice the inconveniences of every day—the weather is too hot or too cold, time passes too quickly or too slowly, there's too much to do or not enough, routine tasks bore us and challenges stress us, the coffee is too weak and the waiting too long. How hard we are to please! How blind to His gifts!

With trust in the Lord, our many blessings come in unexpected forms—hope for the future, truth through the Word, certainty in the Truth, stronger faith with deeper roots, greater peace in times of difficulty, joy in knowing everlasting love. When we trust God in all things, we see His hand in all the details of life. How gently the Holy Spirit whispers in these moments! How sweet are His blessings!

Blessed Redeemer:

You must grow weary of my complaints, expectations, and dissatisfaction. You must wonder why I search in circles of discontent, continuing to miss the blessings right in front of me. You have great patience with me!

My heart always discovers Your blessings when I look for You. I find Your glory in the morning dew on the grass, in the bumble bee pollinating the flowers, and in the magenta sky at sunset. I feel Your kindness in the laughter of a friend and the smile of a stranger, in the tears of a mother and the sleep of a child. I know Your presence when my uncertain times find healing, when my beautiful celebrations offer praise, and when my prayers in all forms rise to You. You give a greater grace. Amen.

PERSONAL REFLECTIONS

THURSDAY

Altar of Holiness

> How lovely is your dwelling place, O LORD of Heaven's Armies. I long, yes, I faint with longing to enter the courts of the LORD. With my whole being, body and soul, I will shout joyfully to the living God. Even the sparrow finds a home, and the swallow builds her nest and raises her young at a place near Your altar, O LORD of Heaven's Armies, my King and my God! What joy for those who can live in your house, always singing your praises.
>
> Psalm 84:1–4 (NLT)

I have learned so much about prayer, especially from reading and rereading *Prayer—Finding the Heart's True Home* by Richard Foster. Foster writes, "God wants us to be present where we are. He invites us to see and hear what is around us and through it all, to discern the footprints of the Holy."[2] As I consider these words, my senses are heightened. He draws me near. I bring everything before Him—not just my needs, but definitely my needs—not just my hopes, but my will—not just my petitions for others, but my belief that He knows what is best for others. Still and quiet, I listen for His whispers, my soul embraced by Perfect Love.

God of the Angel Armies:

I am humbled that You would invite me to enter Your courts, to enter into the Holy of Holies. My soul bows in reverence in Your holy presence. You are Greeting and Benediction, Greatness and Bounty, Goodness and Beauty!

With my whole being, body and soul, I shout praises with joy and gratitude. My body worships You for extravagant provision and protection. My soul knows a contentment at this altar that it cannot find anywhere else. You are Shelter!

King of my heart, I seek wisdom in my prayers, yearning for Your voice. I seek Truth in the Word, yearning for Your direction. Hear my praises and prayers for lavish love and generous grace. You are Joy! Amen.

PERSONAL REFLECTIONS

---

2. Foster, Richard J. *Prayer: Finding the the Heart's True Home* (San Francisco: HarperSan Francisco, 1992), 28.

FRIDAY

Perfector of Endurance

> Therefore, since we are surrounded by such a huge crowd of witnesses to the life of faith, let us strip off every weight that slows us down, especially the sin that so easily trips us up. And let us run with endurance the race God has set before us. We do this by keeping our eyes on Jesus, the champion who initiates and perfects our faith. Because of the joy awaiting him, he endured the cross, disregarding its shame. Now he is seated in the place of honor beside God's throne.
>
> **Hebrews 12:1–2 (NLT)**

In choosing to follow Jesus, we become identified with Him. Be alert! Scripture reminds that many watch us, but some look for an opportunity to point out our weaknesses. God calls us to run with endurance this great race of faith. Because our priorities reveal our faith walk, we must keep the focus on Jesus.

Sin will always try to discourage us, distract us, and defeat us. Despite difficulties, we must endure the journey. Jesus, the champion who initiates and perfects our faith, cheers us on to victory; the world will take last place. We must persevere in our faithfulness to Christ, remembering He endured the cross for our sins.

Jesus, Soul Champion:
How often we think of Your glory and forget the cross!
How often we think of Your love and forget the sacrifice!
How often we think of Your faithfulness and forget the cost!

Jesus, Faith Champion:
Encourage us to stay the course and endure the race.
Let us be faithful witnesses for You. Amen.

※ PERSONAL REFLECTIONS ※

SATURDAY

See Jesus

> Suddenly, Moses and Elijah appeared and began talking with Jesus . . . a bright cloud overshadowed them, and a voice from the cloud said, "This is my dearly loved Son, who brings me great joy. Listen to him." The disciples were terrified and fell face down on the ground. Then Jesus came over and touched them. "Get up," he said. "Don't be afraid." And when they looked up . . . they saw only Jesus.
>
> **Matthew 17: 3, 5–8 (NLT)**

These disciples witnessed an amazing and holy power. God called Jesus His beloved Son, saying, "Listen to him." Jesus said to the disciples, "Don't be afraid." In the presence of God and His holiness they were overwhelmed. Jesus called to them, and when they looked up, they saw only Jesus.

I can feel His holy presence surrounding my desire to trust fully and my inability to comprehend completely. Taking wordless prayers, the Holy Spirit speaks my heart to the Father. God calls me His beloved and reminds me to not be afraid. Whenever I look up, I want to see Jesus.

Jesus, Beloved Son of God:
Like the disciples, I do not always understand Your power. I do not recognize Your plans. I do not grasp Your

message. Like the disciples, I fall down, amazed and awed by Your holiness. I kneel, humble and unworthy of Your compassion. I pray, convicted and wordless through the Spirit. And like the disciples, I find only You—Blessed Assurance. Amen.

PERSONAL REFLECTIONS

Fourth Sunday in Lent

Real Love

> This is how God showed his love to us: He sent his one and only Son into the world so that we could have life through him. This is what real love is: It is not our love for God; it is God's love for us. He sent his Son to die in our place to take away our sins. Dear friends, if God loved us that much we also should love each other.
>
> **1 John 4:9–11 (NCV)**

During this season of renewal, we examine love. In sending Christ, God expresses a greater love than human hearts can offer. "God loved us that much" defines real love, pure and generous, holy and righteous, forgiving and eternal. This is holy love.

Real love exceeds our frail attempts to love. We struggle to love with pure intentions and without expectations, with constant prayer and without judgment, with gentle compassion and without terms. Only through Christ can we really love.

Jesus, Lover of my soul:
   You, being perfect in every way, reach out to me. You, knowing my sinful nature, offer love to me anyway. My mind struggles to grasp this vast measure of divine love.

My heart desires to receive the unknown depths of Your holy love.

You love me with unfailing compassion; I want to love like this.

You love me with boundless grace; I long to love as You love.

You loved me before my first breath; I yearn to love You until my last breath. I ache to know real love, love beyond breathing, love everlasting. Amen.

PERSONAL REFLECTIONS

MONDAY

Good Deeds

> For the grace of God has been revealed . . . We should live in this evil world with wisdom, righteousness, and devotion to God, while we look forward with hope to that wonderful day when the glory of our great God and Savior, Jesus Christ, will be revealed. He gave his life to free us from every kind of sin, to cleanse us, and to make us his very own people, totally committed to doing good deeds.
>
> **Titus 2:11–14 (NLT)**

While eating dinner in a delicatessen on Broadway in New York City, my family and I witness an opportunity for a good deed. A woman offers to buy a homeless man a cookie at the bakery, only to discover she is fifty cents short. After asking several times for the extra change, no one responds. So, we give her the fifty cents. Then, this woman comes to our table, introduces herself, thanks us, and prays over us a genuine, faithful prayer of thanksgiving and blessing for helping.

At first, it seems we had only helped to buy a cookie, but this woman demonstrated what it takes to be used by God:

- recognize a need;
- reach out willingly;

- give without expectations;
- ask for help when needed; and
- be thankful for God's provision.

The lovely woman, who would only identify herself as being "from Brooklyn," offered a random act of kindness for no reward. In her giving, the homeless man received a cookie, but we found a life lesson. I will always remember the beautiful prayer of blessing she stopped to offer Father God.

Father:

Your Word teaches us to live with wisdom, righteousness, and devotion to You. By Your grace alone, we are given the wisdom to see the need, the righteousness to love each other, and the devotion to honor the true God.

To be loved by Jesus, to be cleansed from sin, and to be committed to doing good deeds for His glory identify us as believers. Let our intentions originate in You. Let the world see You in our every good deed. For grace that is greater, let our actions offer thanksgiving to You. Amen.

PERSONAL REFLECTIONS

Tuesday

Splendor of His Love

> [Jesus prayed]:
> Father, it's time. Display the bright splendor of your Son so the Son in turn may show your bright splendor. You put him in charge of everything human so he might give real and eternal life to all in his charge. And this is the real and eternal life: that they know you, the one and only true God, and Jesus Christ, whom you sent. . . . And now, Father, glorify me with your very own splendor, the very splendor I had in your presence before there was a world.
>
> **John 17:1–8**

Here Is Love Vast as the Ocean

Here is love vast as the ocean,
Loving kindness as the flood.
When the Prince of Life, our ransom,
Shed for us His precious blood.
Who His love will not remember?
Who can cease to sing His praise?

He can never be forgotten
Throughout Heaven's eternal days.
On the mount of crucifixion,
Fountains opened deep and wide.

> Through the floodgates of God's mercy,
> Flowed a vast and gracious tide.
>
> Grace and love like mighty rivers
> Poured incessant from above,
> And Heaven's peace and perfect justice
> Kissed a guilty world in love.

I cannot find who wrote these words. The work is listed as "public domain," which leads me to believe they were written as a poem a long time ago and have been put to music.

This song captures my soul again, just like when I heard it for the first time. How beautiful the words and the thoughts— the Prince of Life who is grace and love like mighty rivers! This song embraces my soul with His splendor. I hope this Love vast as the ocean flows into all my moments. I hope His incessant grace brings peace and perfect justice to my days.

True God:

Your splendor shines brightest through Jesus, a Love vast as the ocean. My heart weeps as I ponder Your beauty. I whisper, Yeshua, You are grace poured incessant from above that fills my soul as nothing else. I believe You are the One and only True God. You are Real Life. You are Love Eternal. Amen.

PERSONAL REFLECTIONS

Wednesday

Response to Living Hope

> So here's what I want you to do, God helping you: Take your everyday, ordinary life—your sleeping, eating, going-to-work, and walking-around life—and place it before God as an offering. Embracing what God does for you is the best thing you can do for him. Don't become so well-adjusted to your culture that you fit into it without even thinking. Instead, fix your attention on God. You'll be changed from the inside out. Readily recognize what he wants from you, and quickly respond to it. Unlike the culture around you, always dragging you down to its level of immaturity, God brings the best out of you, develops well-formed maturity in you.
>
> **Romans 12:1–2**

The Scripture above is more familiar in the translations that use phrases like "living sacrifices" and "be transformed by the renewing of your mind," but *The Message* gives us examples of how we are to be these phrases. Becoming too much like the world is a constant danger for us. The power of the world entertains our imaginations, teases our thoughts, and heightens our emotions. Darkness will always lure us down to its level of immaturity. So, how are we to be transformed? We must keep our focus on God, whose "compassions . . . are new every morning; great is your faithfulness" (Lam. 3:19-23 NIV).

Eternal Hope:

I confess that darkness entices me, and each time, I rediscover its illusions of better and happier and wishful. Deceptively, the world veils the truth like a magician, distracting me with a maze of limited results. This is not hope!

Your Word tells me to passionately wait and quietly hope in God. I am to bring the things of my ordinary life and to offer them to the Holy Father. Lovingly and creatively chosen for me, God's purposes are always best. I wait for hope!

Transform me! Make me more like You; change me from the inside out.

Renew me! Find me where I am; pour out Your mercies every day.

Teach me! Give me life lessons that grow faith; develop my perseverance.

Refine me! Take my joys and my burdens; melt me into Your will.

Create me new every day with Your unlimited possibilities!

You are Living Hope! Amen.

PERSONAL REFLECTIONS

THURSDAY

A Living Letter

> The Father . . . takes us to the high places of blessing in him. . . . It's in Christ that we find out who we are and what we are living for . . . It's in Christ that you, once you heard the truth and believed it (this Message of your salvation), found yourselves home free—signed, sealed, and delivered by the Holy Spirit.
>
> **Ephesians 1:3, 11, 13**

Richard Foster reminds us, "Each day in a new and living way the brooding Spirit of God teaches us. As we begin to follow these nudgings of the Spirit, we are changed from the inside out."[3] We are living letters written by the grace of God, letters that are to tell the story of redemption—our own and the world's.

Father of glory:

When I consider the blessings of Your goodness, my list is endless. Even in the darkest night, You take me to those high places of blessing. When my soul needs shelter from the storms of life, You are the safe harbor. When my heart celebrates, You plan the party. When my mind searches for understanding, You send wisdom. In all times, in all ways, Your blessings gather in abundance.

Messiah:

In You I find the reason for being. You were broken and pierced for my sins, that I might be made new. Even in my weakest moment, You still love me. As my soul calls out for direction, You are the Way. As my heart learns compassion, You are the Gentle Shepherd. As my mind needs feeding, You are the Bread of Life. Through sacrifice and through provision, Your grace falls with extravagance.

Author and Finisher of my faith:

In You I am a living letter signed, sealed, and delivered by the Holy Spirit. You are the One who whispers the prayers of my heart to the Most High. If my soul doubts the journey, You renew my hope. If my heart quivers at the task, You remove wasted fears. If my mind hesitates as evil manipulates, You expose the truth. Beyond imagination, beyond forever, Your holiness hovers with boldness.

On my knees, I come to the altar amazed that Almighty God would send abundant blessings to me, that the Deliverer would pour extravagant grace on me, that the Prince of Peace would whisper boldness into me. Perfect Love covers me, and I am complete. Amen.

PERSONAL REFLECTIONS

---

3. Foster, Richard J. *Prayer: Finding the the Heart's True Home* (San Francisco: HarperSan Francisco, 1992), 57.

FRIDAY

How Christ Loves

> Mostly what God does is love you. Keep company with him and learn a life of love. Observe how Christ loved us. His love was not cautious but extravagant. He didn't love in order to get something from us but to give everything of himself to us. Love like that.
>
> **Ephesians 5:2b**

As believers, we are called to live a life of love. How do we learn this? We must spend time with God to learn His definition of love. Perfect Love comes as amazing grace, fragrant and abundant.

To love as Christ, we must be steadfast, selfless, and sincere in our motivations. How can we achieve this? When we keep company with Him through prayer and the study of His Word, a relationship develops. It is in this relationship that He nurtures and nourishes our spiritual growth. As we grow spiritually, we become more like Christ. He loves unconditionally and without measure. Love like that.

Adonai:

You are Divine Love, pure and sincere. The world alters this definition of love, making it selfish and fragile. Finding no satisfaction in such love, we turn away and begin to build walls to separate us from the pain. We choose not to love when we have not experienced real love.

You are holy and true, the One who loved us from the beginning. Through Your perfect love we discover a wholeness that the world does not know. In communion of Spirit and soul, Your presence exceeds words. We experience love with a new heart, with a renewed purpose. The fragrance of this holy love lingers. Let us love like that. Amen.

❦ PERSONAL REFLECTIONS ❧

SATURDAY

Turning Point

> But the story we're given is a God-story not an Abraham-story. What we read in Scripture is, "Abraham entered into what God was doing for him, and that was the turning point. He trusted God to set him right instead of trying to be right on his own."
>
> **Romans 4:2b–3**

In Genesis 15:5–6, this God-story is written:

> Then the LORD took Abram outside and said to him, "Look up into the sky and count the stars if you can. That's how many descendants you will have!" And Abram believed the LORD, and the LORD counted him righteous because of his faith (NLT).

Abraham believed the Lord and the promise God was giving him. This was far beyond his ability to comprehend, but Abraham accepted it by faith. When Abraham entered into what God was doing for him, and embraced God's plan, that was the turning point.

God's promise of forgiveness and life everlasting is a gift from Him and can only be accepted by faith. No matter how many good deeds I do, how many offerings I give, or how many times I pray, these efforts fail to redeem my soul. Only when I place my faith in the Living God, who loves me in ways that are beyond my ability to comprehend, am I declared righteous. God's blessings come when I embrace what He is doing for me, and that is always the turning point.

Yahweh:

You are the LORD of Abraham; You are the Covenant Maker. When I cannot see the purpose of Your way, when I cannot understand the reasons of Your plan, when I cannot comprehend the glory of Your love, remind me to look up into the heavens and count the stars if I can. . . because I cannot.

You are the Lord of my life; You are the Promise Keeper. I desire Your way even when I cannot see Your purpose. I desire Your plan, even when I cannot understand Your reasons. I desire Your love, even when I cannot comprehend Your glory. I desire to live in a faith-embrace with the Living God, so I can tell this God-story. Amen.

PERSONAL REFLECTIONS

FIFTH SUNDAY IN LENT

Living Holiness

> But what happens when we live God's way? He brings gifts into our lives, much the same way that fruit appears in an orchard—things like affection for others, exuberance about life, serenity. We develop a willingness to stick with things, a sense of compassion in the heart, and a conviction that a basic holiness permeates things and people. We find ourselves involved in loyal commitments, not needing to force our way in life, able to marshal and direct our energies wisely.
>
> **Galatians 5:22–23a**

This Scripture examines the gifts that come from living God's way. What is God's way? Earlier in chapter 5 of Galatians we find the answer: "Love others as you love yourself. That's an act of true freedom" (v. 14). We are cautioned not to be selfish or revengeful, rather we are called to "live freely . . . motivated by God's Spirit" (v. 16).

This orchard of fruit comes to us through the Holy Spirit. As we allow the Spirit to lead us in our decisions and to be the intentions of our desires, our relationship with Christ grows deeper. Our focus begins to turn from the world to God. While our sins have been crucified with

Christ, we must move beyond just believing. Becoming more holy is living God's way.

Spirit of God:

The ways of the human heart are selfishness and discontent and envy. These raw emotions defeat us. We get lost in a cycle of wanting and control and misery. Help us find a better way.

The ways of the Spirit are kindness and peace and love. These fruits from Your orchard delight the mind and heart and soul. We can know goodness and joy and gentleness and patience. Help us find Your way!

Walk before us, leading us to the orchard where our hearts can enjoy all the fruits You give. To live in the way of the Spirit is to find His gifts. Help us live God's way. Amen.

※ PERSONAL REFLECTIONS ※

MONDAY

Refined Design

> Be energetic in your life of salvation, reverent and sensitive before God. That energy is God's energy, an energy deep within you, God himself willing and working at what will give him the most pleasure.
>
> **Philippians 2:12b–13**

When I come into the Holy of Holies, my body responds with reverence to God All-Sufficient. Physically and spiritually, I bow before the Sustainer and Savior, the Sanctifier. In His presence there is an energy that overwhelms the human mind, that speaks without language. My soul is known.

Oswald Chambers writes in *My Utmost for His Highest*:

> The most profound thing in a person is his will, not sin. The will is the essential element in God's creation of human beings—sin is a perverse nature which entered into people. In someone who has been born again, the source of the will is the Almighty God.[4]

When I ask God for guidance, God's energy answers. When I seek His good purpose for me, the Creator's will becomes my will. When I am obedient to His prompting, the Counselor illumines my mind. Immanuel abides with me, prodding and providing my every need. There is a knowing in my soul.

Almighty God:

Designed to choose, I sometimes go my own way. Forgive me when I ignore Your details in life and follow the gestures of the world. Refined to choose, my heart knows the consequences of evil. Forgive me when I am attracted to fool's gold and miss Your carbon stones.

Designed to choose, I desire to be obedient to Your purpose. Guide me with Your energy for encouragement and perseverance. Refined to choose, I am being renewed every day with Your mercy. You are God All-Sufficient.

I am designed by Your choice; You have a plan for my life. I am refined by Your choice; take me now. Like carbon which endures extreme pressures and temperatures deep within Your earth, make me a diamond. Remove my impurities. Polish me in ways that will give You the most pleasure. Amen.

❧ PERSONAL REFLECTIONS ☙

---

4. Oswald Chambers, *My Utmost for His Highest: Selections for the Year* (Grand Rapids, MI: Discovery House Publishers, 1989), n.p.

Tuesday
More than Enough

> God is perfectly able to enrich you with every grace, so that you always have enough for every conceivable need, and your resources overflow in all kinds of good work.
>
> 2 Corinthians 9:8 (NJB)

We often limit God by demanding more and expecting less. The heart exclaims its wants and ignores its needs. The soul devours the Scriptures and omits prayer. The mind wrestles with urgency and forgets possibility. Our thoughts are not God's thoughts.

E. M. Bounds writes in his book *E. M. Bounds on Prayer*, "The prayers of holy men are ever streaming up to God, as fragrant as the richest incense." He reminds us that God speaks by "declaring His wealth and our impoverishment."[5] Throughout the Scriptures, God's greatness and faithfulness and justice are revealed. Our prayers must rise to the Great Provider.

Jehovah-Jireh, The Lord our Provider:

I fall victim to the world, craving more than I need. I read the Word, but talk to You by reciting a list of wants. I struggle with the importance of my desires and miss Your possibilities. I limit my blessings. You are limitless.

Let my prayers rise to the Holy One. I am asking for what I need with the certainty that You will provide more than enough. I am praying with inspired words, meditating on the holy words of Scripture. You are everything to my soul—Maker and Defender, Creator and Sustainer, Redeemer and Lover, Hope and Possibility. You are Grace. Amen.

❧ PERSONAL REFLECTIONS ☙

---

5. E. M. Bounds, *E. M. Bounds on Prayer* (New Kensington, PA: Whitaker House, 1997), p. 22.

WEDNESDAY
Everlasting Testimony

> Lord, You have been our dwelling place throughout all generations before the mountains were born or you brought forth the earth and the world, from everlasting to everlasting you are God. . . . May the favor of the Lord our God rest upon us; establish the work of our hands for us—yes, establish the work of our hands.
>
> **Psalm 90:1–2, 17 (NIV)**

The author of Psalm 90 was Moses, which makes this the oldest psalm. The New Living Translation titles the psalm "A prayer of Moses, the man of God." This prayer speaks to the majesty of God as Eternal Creator. Having always been and always to be, God reigns everlasting to everlasting. We remain as created, finite and limited. What a generous gift, this dwelling place!

When I ponder the beauty of the Lord, my words are less than adequate. To see Him in the splendor of the dogwood's blossoms renews my hope. To find Him in the gentle breezes of the mighty wind nurtures my spirit. To know Him in the tender prayer of a caring friend touches my soul. As a dear friend once told me, "Only as spirit testifies with Spirit can these depths of gratitude be understood."

Blessed Assurance:

Even before time began, Your beauty danced across the heavens. From the highest peaks to the deepest canyons, from the widest deserts to the strongest rivers, Your glory shines. From forever to forever, You are Jehovah-Elohim, the Eternal Creator.

Even before I took my first breath, Your plans for me were known. From the sweetest celebrations to the gravest sorrows, from the abundant blessings to the fiercest challenges, Your love abides. From before to after, forever be my dwelling place. Amen.

PERSONAL REFLECTIONS

Thursday

Everything and All

> LORD, you have examined me and know all about me. You know when I sit down and when I get up. You know my thoughts before I think them. You know where I go and where I lie down. You know everything I do. LORD, even before I say a word, you already know it. You are all around me—in front and in back—and have put your hand on me. Your knowledge is amazing to me; it is more than I can understand.
>
> **Psalm 139:1–6 (NCV)**

You made all the delicate, inner parts of my body and knit me together in my mother's womb. Thank you for making me so wonderfully complex! Your workmanship is marvelous—how well I know it. You watched me as I was being formed in utter seclusion, as I was woven together in the dark of the womb. You saw me before I was born. Every day of my life was recorded in your book. Every moment was laid out before a single day had passed.

—Psalm 139:13–16 (NLT)

God, your thoughts are precious to me. They are so many! If I could count them, they would be more than all the grains of sand . . . God, examine me and know my heart;

test me and know my anxious thoughts. See if there is any bad thing in me. Lead me on the road to everlasting life.
—Psalm 139:17–18, 23–24 (NCV)

Faithful Father:

What makes me think I can hide my doubts from You? How can I pretend to be strong when You know I am not? Why would You listen so intently to my prayers when You already know my needs? When am I ever alone?

You know all about me and love me still. I am never alone—You are all around me. You listen to the groans of my soul with mercy and tenderness. You are my strength; You make me bold, for I am nothing without You. Lord, even before I say a word, my heart's desires, my anxious thoughts, my hurried spirit, my silent fears—all are known. You are too marvelous for me!

You create magnificent designs, each one unique. Your thoughts are like threads of gold and silver and cotton and silk, in colors of every shade, while our moments are like remnants of fibers with varied hues and textures and patterns. Your thoughts and our moments are woven and spun into holy tapestries of love. With majesty and grace, You weave them together for glory-purposes that exceed my abilities to know or understand. God, examine me, lead me—in all things, at all times! Amen.

❧ PERSONAL REFLECTIONS ☙

FRIDAY

Fruitful Harvest

> And the seeds that fell on the good soil represent honest, good-hearted people who hear God's word, cling to it, and patiently produce a huge harvest.
>
> **Luke 8:15 (NLT)**

In the eighth chapter of Luke, Jesus tells the parable of the Four Soils to a large crowd. Then Jesus explains the parable when His disciples asked what the story meant. The four soils—a footpath, shallow soil with underlying rock, thorny ground, and fertile soil—represent the types of people who hear the Good News. Not all hear and only some believe!

In verses 11–15 of chapter 9, Jesus gives examples of each kind of soil by describing the personal responses to hearing the Gospel message. Some choose not to believe, while others follow Jesus but never place their faith in Him. There are those whose lives are too full of themselves and their own desires to follow Jesus. And lastly, the good soil represents those who choose Jesus, follow Him, and share the Good News. Because of these honest, good-hearted people, many will hear and believe.

Lord of the Harvest:

Listening to the story, we realize that some hear and do not believe, some do not hear, some are too full of the world;

but some do hear and will believe and must tell. You are the Farmer, the Sower of seeds, planting the Good News.

Let me be fertile soil. Let the seeds of truth be planted in me; let me grow the seeds of faith. Let me plant new crops. You will nourish them with prevailing sunshine and necessary rains. The harvests will be plentiful, fields of righteousness and bounty-full grace. You are Lord of the Harvest! Amen.

❧ PERSONAL REFLECTIONS ❧

SATURDAY
In His Hand

> But ask the animals, and they will teach you; the birds of the air, and they will tell you; ask the plants of the earth, and they will teach you; and the fish of the sea will declare to you. Who among all these does not know that the hand of the Lord has done this? In his hand is the life of every living thing and the breath of every human being.
>
> Job 12:7–10 (NRSV)

Zophar suggests that Job has secret sins, and God, knowing all things, must be punishing him for these. Job knows God to be all-knowing and all-powerful and everywhere. His response in the verses above expresses his belief that God is Creator. Regardless of Job's personal circumstances and his situational uncertainty, he concludes that every living thing on the earth is in His hand.

We, like Zophar, try to examine life with its dilemmas and choices, its disasters and consequences, its diseases and cures. The reasons scream for explanation while reality whispers disbelief. We, like Job, must acknowledge God as Creator and Sustainer of all life. To remember this we need only to look at His creations. God holds us in His hand at all times, in all things, through all trials.

Holy Father:

In times when we do not understand, we question and doubt Your power, presence, and purpose. Lacking the wisdom to explain, we debate and dilute Your image into a powerless and revengeful entity. We dishonor You.

Forgive our arrogant gestures and prideful excuses. Forgive our narrow views and shallow thoughts. Forgive our irreverent attempts to define You. Forgive us when we fail to see You as God All-Sufficient, Eternal Creator, Enduring Love.

Your ways exceed our thoughts; Your purposes transcend our vision. The hand of the Lord is in all things—before time and after time, yesterday and tomorrow, the present age and generations to come. Every living thing bears Your fingerprints. You alone are all we need. You are the breath within each of us. You are Everlasting Hope! Amen.

PERSONAL REFLECTIONS

PALM SUNDAY

Glorious Hope

> . . . All of his followers began to shout and sing as they walked along, praising God for all the wonderful miracles they had seen.
> "Blessings on the King who comes in the name of the LORD! Peace in heaven, and glory in highest heaven!"
> But some of the Pharisees among the crowd said, "Teacher, rebuke your followers for saying things like that!"
> [Jesus] replied, "If they kept quiet, the stones along the road would burst into cheers!"
> But as he came closer to Jerusalem and Jesus saw the city ahead, he began to weep.
>
> Luke 19:37b–41 (NLT)

Crowds filled the roadside, children sang songs, and joyful cheers rang loud. As Jesus passed, the crowds waved palm branches. Many shouted God-songs for miracles and wonders they had witnessed: "Bless the King who comes in the name of the Lord! Peace in heaven and glory in the highest heaven!"

Similar words had welcomed Jesus before this day. The angels announced the birth of the Messiah with glory-songs and peace-filled praises.

> Suddenly, the angel was joined by a vast host of others— the armies of heaven—praising God and saying,

"Glory to God in the highest heaven, and peace on earth to those with whom God is pleased."
—Luke 2:13–14 (NLT)

The world expected a different savior, one who would be king, or deliver them from oppressive rulers. They hoped for political glory. But the Holy One came as the Savior, the King of kings, the Deliverer. He remains the Hope that brings eternal glory. When Jesus saw the city, He began to mourn for His people, knowing God's righteous judgment to come.

Anointed One:

You are Messiah and Savior and Son. Welcomed by angels singing "Glory to God in the highest heavens," the people were amazed but did not understand.

You are Prophet and Priest and King. Cheered by crowds shouting "Glory in the highest heaven," the people were amazed but did not understand.

You are Christ and Redeemer and Risen Lord. Rejected by the world saying "Crucify! Crucify!," You amaze us with forgiveness and reconciliation.

You are Living Water and Bread of life and Prince of Peace. Cherished by believers telling Your glory-story, You amaze us with provision and compassion.

You are Eternal Hope and Everlasting Faithfulness and Enduring Love. Defined by Glory rising "Peace be with you," You are Amazing Grace! Amen.

PERSONAL REFLECTIONS

MONDAY

Pierced Righteousness

> But he was pierced for our transgressions,
>   he was crushed for our iniquities;
>   the punishment that brought us peace was upon him,
>   and by his wounds we are healed.
>
> **Isaiah 53:5 (NIV)**

When he sees all that is accomplished by his anguish,
  he will be satisfied.
And because of his experience,
  my righteous servant will make it possible for many to be counted righteous,
  for he will bear all their sins.

—Isaiah 53:11 (NLT)

This prophecy about the Messiah depicts a servant who will not be stranger to grief or disappointment. He will know rejection and harsh treatment. The words in Isaiah 53 describe a servant full of humility and willing to be an offering for sin. Called God's righteous servant, Jesus would bear all their sins, but He had done no wrong.

The people of Israel did not understand these words. Centuries later, we still struggle with these truths. Why would the Word Incarnate be pierced for *my* sins? While the cross personifies the sins of all people and the darkness in every heart, we weep at the suffering Jesus endured—the rejection, the accusations, the beatings, the nails, the thorns. By His grace, through faith we are made righteous; by "His wounds we are healed."

Meshiach (Hebrew word for "Messiah"):

You are the long-awaited Messiah, the Word made flesh. The world was not kind to You; it did not see Your beauty and did not accept Your truth. Righteous Servant, they nailed You to a cross. You became the Passover Lamb, one sacrifice for all. Because of me, You were pierced.

You are the Holy One. Forgive me when I forget the wounds You wore for me. Forgive me when I forget the thorns You wore for me. Forgive me when I forget the nails You wore for me. Because of You, I am forgiven. Because of You, I am made new. Because of You, I wear a robe of righteousness. Amen.

PERSONAL REFLECTIONS

TUESDAY

Perfect Lamb

> They are to take some of the blood and smear it on the sides and top of the doorframes of the houses where they eat the animal. That same night they must roast the meat over a fire and eat it along with bitter salad greens and bread made without yeast.... On that night I will pass through the land of Egypt and strike down every firstborn son and firstborn male animal in the land of Egypt. I will execute judgment against all the gods of Egypt, for I am the LORD! But the blood on your doorposts will serve as a sign, marking the houses where you are staying. When I see the blood, I will pass over you.
>
> Exodus 12:7–8, 12–13a (NLT)

God was to set the Israelites free from their bondage of servitude after 430 years in Egypt. Specific instructions of how to prepare the lamb and mark their homes were given to the Israelites. There was much symbolism in these details, but the greatest was sacrificing an unblemished lamb whose blood would be a sign for the Lord to spare them. Still today, every year the Jewish people celebrate Passover in remembrance of God's deliverance from Egypt and His unfailing promises.

Jerusalem was preparing for the Passover observance when Jesus returned. According to *Mounce's Complete*

Expository Dictionary of Old and New Testament Words, at the time Jesus was being crucified, "the Passover lamb was being slain in the temple."[6] On the cross, Jesus became the sacrificed Lamb, the Most Holy, the absolute atonement that frees us from our bondage to sin and spiritual death. His blood became the sign of redemption for believers. Each time believers gather for the Lord's Supper, our Passover feast, we remember our deliverance from sin and His promises fulfilled.

Lamb of God:

When I think of You at the table during the Last Supper, sitting with Your beloved disciples, the emotions must have been legion. Aware the time was near, You must have felt sadness at parting. Perhaps You wondered if they would continue the ministry. There was the brokenness of Your heart, knowing the coming betrayal by one of the disciples. They did not understand all the words You spoke, all the truths You revealed. They did not understand why You took on the role of a servant, why You washed their feet. Is that how You find me, too?

There are times I just don't understand the purposes, cannot figure out Your plan. Sometimes, I just don't listen and do not hear the whispers of truth. When the world questions or minimizes my beliefs and I compromise or deny my faith, my actions or silence betrays You. Often times, I struggle with the servant role.

Like Your beloved disciples who watched You betrayed, beaten, and broken, I am familiar with Your story. While I did not sit by the sea hearing Your lessons or walk along the dusty road following You to Jerusalem, I know Your presence and feel a yearning deep inside when You draw near and illumine my mind and heart and soul with Your Word.

You are the Living Sacrifice that testifies for redemption. You are the Lamb of God whose blood purchased my deliverance. You are Divine Love full of mercy. And—You call me beloved. Amen.

PERSONAL REFLECTIONS

---

6. William D. Mounce, ed., *Mounce's Complete Expository Dictionary of Old and New Testament Words* (Grand Rapids, MI: Zondervan, 2006), p. 500.

WEDNESDAY

Betrayed

> Then Judas Iscariot, one of the twelve disciples, went to the leading priests and asked, "How much will you pay me to betray Jesus to you?" And they gave him thirty pieces of silver. From that time on, Judas began looking for an opportunity to betray Jesus.
>
> Matthew 26:14–16 (NLT)

> So Judas came straight to Jesus. "Greetings, Rabbi!" he exclaimed and gave him the kiss.
>
> —Matthew 26:49 (NLT)

*B*etrayal carries a dark stigma. Perhaps the sting is worse when it comes from a friend. Such is Judas' betrayal of Christ. Psalm 41:9 speaks in prophecy of this: "Even my close friend in whom I trusted, who ate my bread, has lifted up his heel against me" (NASB). Judas betrays Christ for the price of a slave, thirty pieces of silver. How do I betray Christ?

Jesus asks the disciples, "Don't you realize that I could ask my Father for thousands of angels to protect us, and he would send them instantly?" (Matt. 26:53 NLT).

While the disciples want to stop His arrest, Jesus does not resist. Even His arrest is under Sovereign control. Jesus purposely goes to the cross, and I am freed by Perfect Love. And for *me*, He sends the angels. How often do I misunderstand His Sovereign power?

Deliverer:

That night at dinner, You knew Judas would betray You. You could have stopped him but did not. When he came to You in the garden, You knew his kiss to be a sign of betrayal. You could have called thousands of angels, but You did not. To be in the will of the Father, You willingly went to the cross, betrayed and bruised and broken. You did this for me.

When I am careless at another's expense, my heart is given thirty pieces of silver. When I ignore a need in my abundance, my heart is given thirty pieces of silver. When I do not pray with pure intentions, my heart is given thirty pieces of silver. When I fail to love in Your name, my heart is given thirty pieces of silver. I betray You all the time. Take away my Judas heart! Redeem my heart purchases!

Jesus, I pray to see others through Your eyes, to love like You love. Remind me when I forget to look, when I lack compassion. You are Holy and Sovereign. I long to completely trust in You, the Great Protector. "Angels listen as I sing my thanks" (Ps. 138:1). Amen.

❧ PERSONAL REFLECTIONS ☙

MAUNDY THURSDAY

Perfect Love Intercedes

> Now I am coming to you. I have told them many things while I was with them so they would be filled with my joy. I have given them your word. And the world hates them because they do not belong to the world, just as I do not belong to the world. I'm not asking you to take them out of the world, but to keep them safe from the evil one. They do not belong to this world any more than I do. Make them holy by your truth . . . as you sent me into the world, I am sending them into the world. And I give myself as a holy sacrifice for them so they can be made holy by your truth.
>
> **John 17:13–19 (NLT)**

After breaking the bread and blessing the wine, Jesus tries to explain to the disciples His time is short. Jesus gives them a new commandment: "Love each other. Just as I have loved you, you should love each other. Your love for one another will prove to the world that you are my disciples" (John 13:34b–35 NLT).

Jesus teaches them about the Holy Spirit, the Counselor who will never leave them. He tells them the harsh realities of the world. Then, Jesus prays.

This includes a special prayer for the disciples. Jesus, the Eternal Intercessor, is always the Advocate to God for believers. Jesus knows the world is not kind to His followers and asks the Father for safety from the evil one. He asks the Father to make them pure and holy using the truth in the Word, then sends them into the world to tell God's story. We are today's disciples. Jesus still intercedes.

Father:

Jesus prays that I would find joy in an intimate relationship with You, that I would study Your Word with a hunger and thirst for more. Jesus asks for protection from the evil one because He knows how deceptively evil intrudes. Jesus knows I need to live in the world in order to witness to the world, so He prays for purity and holiness. He knows that Your truth is found in the Word. In yielding to the cross, Jesus repaired the bridge between man and God that sin had destroyed. Jesus invites me to come back home.

Remember the last words of His prayer: "O righteous Father, the world doesn't know you, but I do; and these disciples know you sent me. I have revealed you to them, and I will continue to do so. Then your love for me will be in them, and I will be in them" (John 17:25–26 NLT).

O righteous Father, I know You, and I know that You sent Jesus. He opens my eyes. He illumines my mind and transforms my heart. He kindles a fire that burns within my soul. O Perfect Love, be in me. Amen.

PERSONAL REFLECTIONS

GOOD FRIDAY

Amazing Love

> And when Jesus had cried out again in a loud voice, he gave up his spirit. At that moment the curtain of the temple was torn in two from top to bottom. The earth shook and the rocks split. . . . When the centurion and those with him who were guarding Jesus saw the earthquake and all that had happened, they were terrified, and exclaimed, "Surely he was the Son of God!"
>
> **Matthew 27:50–51, 54 (NIV)**

The curtain in the Temple separated the Holy Place from the Holy of Holies. Only the high priest could enter the Holy of Holies, and only once a year on the Day of Atonement. When Jesus died, this curtain was torn in two from top to bottom. This symbolic act declared there was no longer a barrier between the people and God. Now, each believer becomes a priest who can come into the presence of God, The Holy One.

The Lamb of God became the complete atonement for sin. Jesus is the Lamb slain before the foundation of the world. From the beginning, God's plan included redemption for humanity. Such is this amazing love, beyond our comprehension. When the unexpected happens, we often become perplexed or terrified. We look around for help, answers, or reasons, but we must look for Amazing Love. Because Jesus suffered the agony of the cross, we can go to the altar of the Most High.

Adonai:

This is the day that mourns the agony of the crucifixion. This is the day that breaks my heart. This is the day I reflect upon my sins that required immense pain. This is the day I must remember "by his wounds we are healed" (Isa. 53:5 NIV).

With each act of disobedience, I strike You with a leather whip that breaks the skin. With each untrusting doubt, I push the crown of thorns deeper into Your head. My incessant whining and complaining, selfish pride, and self-righteous anger weigh heavy on Your shoulders as You carry the cross. It is not enough that I ignore You—I mock You and curse You, then deny You. With each fruitless thought, I pound the iron spikes into Your flesh. I am more than ashamed. I hear again the ancient words—"by his wounds we are healed."

How can it be that You would die for me? How could You love me that much? How can I be holy? How could it be that You seek me? You call my name and by Your wounds, I am healed.

I kneel at the altar of the Most High. Your presence embraces me. Repentant tears cleanse my heart. Oh, sweet Jesus, You were broken that I might be made whole. Grace renews my soul. In the presence of Amazing Love, there are no more words. Amen.

PERSONAL REFLECTIONS

SATURDAY

Rest and Restoration

> As his body was taken away, the women from Galilee followed and saw the tomb where his body was placed. Then they went home and prepared spices and ointments to anoint his body. But by the time they were finished the Sabbath had begun, so they rested as required by the law.
>
> Luke 23:55–56 (NLT)

Jesus was placed in a borrowed tomb before sundown on a Friday. In fact, Jewish law required that all preparations for the Sabbath be completed before sundown on Friday so that no work was done on Saturday. The Scriptures do not say anything about that Sabbath. The Bible is silent about who was where or what was said. The only reference is that the women who had gathered the spices to prepare Jesus' body rested all that day as was required of them by the law. There would have been no work on the Sabbath, no traveling to the tomb, and no burial rituals performed.

As I think on that unrecorded day, my thoughts turn to the disciples. They may have been in shock over what had happened and how fast. They may have rested according to the law, but I can only believe their hearts were burdened with questions: if He was the Son of God, why did He die? And what about all the miracles—all the healings and the power? These believers who had followed Jesus, His closest companions, must have pondered the lessons He taught them. What did we not understand? Was it true what he taught us? They must have been disillusioned and weary, afraid, and heartbroken.

Faithful Father:

At times I struggle to understand; my tears seek release. Sometimes, my heart is disillusioned and my soul feels weary. You know all my sorrows, my doubts. Teach my heart a new song.

> Drop Thy still dews of quietness,
> Till all our strivings cease;
> Take from our souls the strain and stress,
> And let our ordered lives confess,
> The beauty of Thy peace.[7]

Some would say that the disciples acted like cowards, while others might say that their love lacked loyalty. Others would suggest that the disciples just did not understand what had really happened, and yet others might suggest that their faith was weak. I cannot know their thoughts or explain their responses. What I do believe is that I am just like them—no braver or more loyal, no wiser or more faithful. What I long to be is more like You—knowing You are the Source of all strength and Your Love endures forever, knowing You are

Wisdom and Your faithfulness never fails. Find me on my knees—repentant at the foot of the cross, reconciled at the altar of the Most High, renewed in the hope of the Spirit. Amen.

❧ PERSONAL REFLECTIONS ☙

7. John Greenleaf Whittier, "Dear Lord and Father of Mankind," 1872.

Easter Sunday
Kindled Soul, Holy Fire

> They said to each other, "Did not our hearts burn within us as he talked to us on the road and explained the scriptures to us?"
>
> Luke 24:32 (NJB)

In the twenty-fourth chapter of Luke, two friends are leaving Jerusalem on the road to Emmaus. It is the morning of the Resurrection. Jesus begins to walk along the road with them, but they do not recognize Him. He talks to them teaching from the Scriptures; still not knowing who He is, they ask Him to stay with them and have dinner. After He blesses the bread, breaks it, and gives it to them, they recognize Him. His presence kindles a fire within their hearts! (13–35).

On Easter morning we hear believers echo, "Christ is risen! Christ is risen indeed!" How do we recognize Him? We are quick to list what we believe, the truths and hopes in the Scriptures of this God-story. But how do we really know it is Him? We can claim the behaviors of religion—confession, forgiveness, baptism, communion, worship, offering, prayer, and study. Does His presence cause your heart to burn within?

In his famous writing, *The Fire of Love*, author Richard Rolle describes when he first felt his heart begin to warm to the Lord.

> I was astonished in the way the heat surged up . . . But once I realized that it came entirely from within, that this fire of love . . . was the gift of my Maker, I was absolutely delighted, and wanted my love to be even greater. And this longing was all the more urgent because of the delightful effect and the interior sweetness which this spiritual flame fed into my soul."[8]

This spiritual flame, the fire burning in the heart of a believer is Amazing Love. Have you had an Emmaus Road experience with the Risen Christ? Can you feel your heart burn in the presence of the Lord? My prayer is that you will know Christ's amazing love.

Holy Fire:

This Resurrection day, believers gather to celebrate New Life. They celebrate victory over sin and death! You are the Risen Christ! We are called to "Go" and share this Good News with the world, this enduring love and eternal life. You only know one way to love. You only know one way to give. You are Amazing Love! You are Extravagant Grace!

Hallelujah! Hallelujah! Praises to the Living God! You are Holy Fire! Spiritual Flame, burn within our souls that we may know Your presence! Be the consuming fire that refines us, making us pure and holy for You. "Baruch Hashem Adonai!" "Blessed be the name of the Lord." You are Everlasting Glory! Amen.

❧ PERSONAL REFLECTIONS ☙

---

8. Richard Rolle, *The Fire of Love*, trans. Clifton Wolters (Harmondsworth: Penguin, 1972), n.p.

About the Author

Donna Oswalt has authored poetry, prayers, and essays, many of which she has published on her inspirational blog *Breathing Room for My Soul* (dhosoulchat.blogspot.com). A Christian since a young age, she has held leadership positions in church including youth and adult Sunday school teacher, discipleship training, and women's Bible studies.

She is currently working on a series of inductive Bible studies and is cofounder of Mangrove Ministries, Inc., a new women's ministry.

A native Mississippian, Oswalt earned a degree in physical therapy and also lived in many parts of the United States and Guam during her husband's career in the U.S. Navy. She currently lives in Mississippi with her husband; they have two daughters.

Kindled Soul, Holy Fire is her first book.